WELCOME TO BOXING BIOGRAPHIES FOR KIDS

Paragon Publishing offers a wide selection of other sports biographies and quiz books, so be sure to check them out if you enjoy this one

Paragon Publishing is a pri company which cares greatly about the accuracy of its content.

As many facts and figures in this book are subject to change, please email us at **ParagonPublishing23@gmail.com** if you notice any inaccuracies to help us keep our book as up-to-date and as accurate as possible.

Enjoy!

CONTENTS

INTRODUCTION

This book will take a look at the 25 greatest boxers of all time. You will learn how each of these boxing legends got into the sport as a child, and then all of the great things that they achieved over their careers. Some of these boxers were around a very long time ago so there may even be names that you do not recognise, or do not know much about.

Before we delve into some of the greatest boxers to ever fight, let us take a brief look at the history of boxing, and how the sport got to be where it is today. Boxing is one of the oldest sports known to man, and people have found 2000 year old paintings in the tombs in Egypt showing that people boxed as long as 5000 years ago!

Boxing was very popular in Ancient Greece, where two fighters would have their hands bound by leather and they would box until someone was knocked out. The Romans were also big boxing fans, however it was banned in 393 AD because it was seen as too savage.

There was very little boxing for the next two thousand years, but it finally started making a comeback amongst the rich in early 16th century London. The boxers would settle disputes among themselves in this way, and other wealthy patrons would put down large wagers on the fights, which is where the term 'prizefighters' was first used.

Fast forward to the 18th century, and a man called Jack Broughton would revolutionize the sport of boxing. He was the first person to introduce a boxing school, as well as creating the first set of boxing rules and mufflers (old version of boxing gloves). Before this there were no real rules, and things like headbutting, chokes, hard throws, and eye-gouging were all allowed.

The Marquess of Queensberry rules were introduced in 1867 and this finally made the sport look like what it does today. This brought an end to bare knuckle boxing, and padded gloves had to be used in all official fights after this, and the rest is history.

Boxing very quickly grew from a chaotic sport without many rules to become one of the biggest sports in the world. Today there are approximately 6.5 million people who regularly train or compete in boxing worldwide and this number is only getting bigger.

From all the millions of people who have ever taken part in the great sport, this book has selected the 25 greatest boxers of all time. Being called one of the GOAT's (Greatest Of All Time) is a very big claim to make and there are many factors that must be ticked for a boxer to even be considered in this bracket. It is not just the number of knockouts that they have achieved over their careers, or the number of fights that they have won, but it is about consistently staying at the top for years or even decades, delivering on the big stage, and leaving a legacy upon the sport.

MUHAMMAD ALI

Nicknames	The Greatest, The People's Champion
Nationality	American
Weight(s)	Heavyweight
Height	1.91 m (6 ft 3 in)
Stance	Orthodox

FIRST FIGHT 1960

RETIRED 1981

TOTAL FIGHTS	61

WINS	WINS BY KO	LOSSES	DRAWS
56	37	5	0

BIOGRAPHY

Cassius Marcellus Clay was born in Louisville, Kentucky on the 17th of January 1942, during an era of racial and political tension. These issues would follow him throughout his life. In 1964 he converted to Islam and changed his name to Muhammad Ali.

When 12-year-old Ali wanted to beat up a thief who had stolen his bicycle, a police officer instead directed him to a boxing gym.

After becoming an amateur boxer in 1954, Ali won the local and national Golden Gloves tournaments. It was already clear that he was a special talent and Ali was picked to represent the United States in the 1960 Olympic Games in Rome. Fighting at light-heavyweight, Ali arrived home victorious with the gold medal. He later told a reporter that he had thrown his medal into a river after receiving racist treatment. Nobody was sure whether this was true as Ali enjoyed playing with the press and feeding them stories.

After winning his Olympic gold medal, Ali turned professional. His record was 19-0 when he stepped up to fight for the heavyweight championship of the world in 1964. At this point, both heavyweight titles were held by a fearsome puncher named Charles 'Sonny' Liston who had won and defended the belts with first-round knockouts.

Ali defeated Liston when the champion quit on his stool with an injured shoulder. Ali beat Liston again in a rematch with a "phantom punch" that many people do not believe landed.

In 1966 Ali was stripped of his world titles when he refused to go and fight in the Vietnam War. He did not fight for nearly four years because of his stance and beliefs. Ali still went on to have a tremendous career. He fought heavyweight rival 'Smokin' Joe Frazier three times. Frazier was the first man to beat Ali. Muhammad won the rematch and, in 1975, they fought for a third time in the Philippines. It was labelled 'The Thrilla in Manila' and Ali won when Frazier's corner retired him after round 14.

Ali also fought Ken Norton three times, losing the first and winning the next two. All three fights with Norton were very close. In 1974 Ali pulled off one of boxing's biggest wins by knocking out George Foreman in Zaire. 60,000 people were in attendance, and it was called 'The Rumble in the Jungle'.

Ali fought on too long and by the time of his last bout in 1981 many fans were concerned about his health. Ali suffered from Parkinson's disease later in life. This dramatically affected his mobility in the years before his death in 2016, aged 74.

Ali fought in many countries around the world, such as Japan, Ireland, Great Britain, Malaysia and Germany. He had two sons and seven daughters including Laila who later became a boxer, as did his Grandson Nico Ali Walsh.

Muhammad Ali will be remembered as not only one of the greatest boxers of all time but as one of the most famous sporting stars.

TRAR

SAUL ALVAREZ

Nicknames	Canelo
Nationality	Mexican
Weight(s)	Light welterweight, Welterweight, Light middleweight, Middleweight, Super middleweight, Light heavyweight
Height	1.74 m (5 ft 8½ in)
Stance	Orthodox

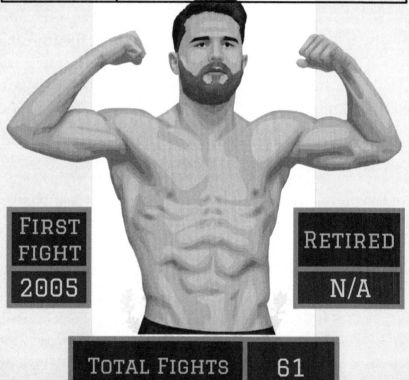

FIRST FIGHT
2005

RETIRED
N/A

TOTAL FIGHTS	61

WINS	WINS BY KO	LOSSES	DRAWS
57	39	2	2

BIOGRAPHY

Santos Saul Alvarez Barragan was born on the 18th of July 1990 in Guadalajara, Mexico. Known worldwide as Canelo, the Mexican star had six brothers who all became professional boxers. This led the youngest member of the family into the sport.

Fighting off bullies as a youngster, Canelo enjoyed early amateur success at the Junior Mexican tournaments and decided to punch for pay. His lifelong trainers Chepo Reynoso and son Eddy Reynoso struggled to find their fighter suitable opponents and he became a pro at just 15 years old.

Apart from a draw in 2006 against Jorge Juarez, Canelo improved nicely and had 35 wins on his record when he beat Ricky Hatton's brother Matthew for the world title in 2011. It was the first world title win of many.

Canelo went on to make six defences of that WBC super-welterweight title, beating good fighters like Shane Mosley and Austin Trout, before suffering his first loss, to Floyd Mayweather Jr. Canelo bounced back with some wins before beating Miguel Cotto at middleweight, drawing with generational rival Gennady Golovkin and beating him in the rematch. In 2019, Canelo knocked out Sergey Kovalev to become a world champion at light-heavyweight.

He had previously won a version of the world titles at super-middleweight, and he decided that 168 was his new home. Victories over Callum Smith and Billy Joe Saunders added two more titles to his cabinet.

In November 2021 Canelo unified the entire super-middleweight division when he knocked out rival Caleb Plant in 11 rounds. Taking Plant's IBF belt, he added to the other three titles he already owned and became an undisputed champion.

Across his career Canelo has made a habit of defeating UK fighters. As well as getting wins over Hatton, Saunders and Callum Smith he also beat Smith's brother Liam plus Amir Khan, Ryan Rhodes and Rocky Fielding.

He has defeated Mexican rivals Alfredo Angulo and Julio Cesar Chavez Jr. Not afraid to take on a challenge, in 2014 many people thought Canelo would avoid Cuba's Erislandy Lara, but he faced him and won on points. Canelo also knocked out James Kirkland in a power-punching firefight and Brooklyn's 'Miracle Man' Daniel Jacobs.

As he became a superstar the Mexican was promoted by former multiple world champion Oscar De La Hoya before they fell out and Canelo set up his own company. Canelo was already a four-weight champion having won titles at 154 pounds, 160 pounds, 168 pounds and as high as 175 pounds. Some even think he can climb as high as cruiserweight or heavyweight given his powerful frame.

As he grew older and gained more fighting experience, Canelo became a classy counter puncher who would wait for his opponents to throw shots and then catch them with heavy blows to head and body.

Alvarez's commonly used nickname 'Canelo' is derived from the Spanish word for Cinnamon and references his striking red hair. A keen golfer, who takes part in celebrity tournaments, Canelo also enjoys horse riding on his Mexican ranch.

MANNY PACQUIAO

Nicknames	Pac Man
Nationality	Filipino
Weight(s)	Flyweight, Super bantamweight, Featherweight, Super featherweight, Lightweight, Light welterweight, Welterweight, Light middleweight
Height	1.66 m (5 5ft ½ in)
Stance	Southpaw

FIRST FIGHT

1995

RETIRED

2001

TOTAL FIGHTS	72

WINS	WINS BY KO	LOSSES	DRAWS
62	39	8	2

BIOGRAPHY

Manny Pacquiao was born as Emmanuel Dapidran Pacquiao on the 17th of December 1978 in Bukidnon, Philippines. Pacquiao dropped out of high school and ended up looking for work in Manila, living on the streets without food. His rise to boxing glory is a true rags-to-riches tale.

Pacquiao started boxing under the guidance of his uncle, in a homemade boxing gym. Fighting was a way of survival and he boxed amateur, being recognised as one of the top Junior boxers in his region.

Manny turned professional in 1996, aged just 16. He won titles in his native Philippines but struggled to make boxing's lowest weights. After making his American debut in 2001 he won the IBF super-bantamweight title and never looked back.

There were roadblocks and disappointments along the way, but he moved up and collected more titles, beating top names every year. Pacquiao defeated 22 world champions in total. This list included the likes of Marco Antonio Barrera who Pacquiao defeated twice. He also defeated Erik Morales twice after losing the first fight against 'El Terrible'. Manny boxed his great rival Juan Manuel Marquez four times, drawing the first, winning the following two and getting dramatically knocked out in the fourth.

Pacquiao also knocked out Ricky Hatton, dominated a weight-drained Oscar De La Hoya in the 'Golden Boy's' final ever fight and stopped Miguel Cotto in the final round. Pacquiao gained revenge on Timothy Bradley twice, after controversially losing their first meeting. He also beat world championship fighters

Antonio Margarito, 'Sugar' Shane Mosley and Lucas Matthysse.

Pacquiao lost the fight of the century to long-time rival Floyd Mayweather Jr in 2015. He bounced back to defeat Adrien Broner and Keith Thurman before losing the final fight of his career, in 2021 to Yordenis Ugas.

Pacquiao's style was slightly changed by his coach Freddie Roach to be more effective. Pacquiao always had very fast hand speed, good footwork and great selection of shots. Respected boxing historian Bert Sugar rated him as the greatest southpaw of all time.

During a 26-year career he moved up through the divisions from light-flyweight to super-welterweight. His lowest recorded weight to highest was a difference of 41 pounds.

The last time he boxed in his native land was against Oscar Larios in 2006. Despite travelling to Malaysia, Australia and twice to Macao in his later years, Pacquiao would never return to the Philippines for a glorious homecoming. Bob Arum's Top Rank organisation promoted many of his biggest fights.

Manny Pacquiao won world titles across four decades. 12 of his major championship wins came across eight divisions. He has previously been named Fighter of the Decade for his work in the 2000s and regularly wins awards for his knockout finishes and general sporting achievements.

A deeply religious person, Pacquiao has spent many years campaigning politically and was formally elected as a Filipino senator in 2016. Even during his boxing career Pacquiao enlisted in military service and climbed the ranks for three years while also competing at the highest level.

JOE LOUIS

Nicknames	The Brown Bomber
Nationality	American
Weight(s)	Heavyweight
Height	1.87 m (6 ft 1½ in)
Stance	Orthodox

FIRST FIGHT 1934

RETIRED 1951

TOTAL FIGHTS	69

WINS	WINS BY KO	LOSSES	DRAWS
66	52	3	0

BIOGRAPHY

Joe Louis was born as Joseph Louis Barrow on the 13th of May 1914 in LaFayette, Alabama. Louis was born in painful poverty with slavery in his family tree. As a youngster, Joe's mother wanted him to learn a musical instrument, so he hid his boxing gloves in a violin case.

Louis picked up the sport quickly. In 1934 he won light-heavyweight gold at the Golden Gloves and later that year the US National Championships. Growing fast, displaying a solid left jab and fierce punching power, Louis knocked out nearly all his 50 amateur victims. Turning professional in 1934 Louis won his first fight by first-round KO which was a sign of things to come.

It was a difficult time for black fighters to get title shots so Louis relied on his manager and trainer to land him an opportunity. They advised him to live clean and present a perfect public image to the media. The first big name on Louis' record was Primo Carnera. Born in Italy, Carnera was a former world champion known as the 'Ambling Alp'. At 6'5" and 260 pounds, Carnera was a giant man for the time. Louis knocked him out in six rounds.

He got closer to a world title shot by first knocking out former world title holder Max Baer and later Paulino Uzcudun. Both tough men were knocked out in four rounds as Louis signalled his severe punch power.

Louis had his first bout against Max Schmeling in 1936. Some thought the German was past his best, but Schmeling trained hard and knocked Louis out in round 12 to hand the

'Brown Bomber' his first loss. That exciting clash was later voted as the 1936 Fight of the Year.

Joe Louis rebuilt with a string of wins before knocking out James J. Braddock for the world heavyweight title. He then embarked on a tremendous run of defences, that included a one-round revenge win over Max Schmeling in 1938.

Louis retired in 1948 after two wins over the excellent Jersey Joe Walcott. He returned in 1950 but lost to Ezzard Charles and finally to Rocky Marciano. The eighth-round knockout loss to Marciano for the world heavyweight title in 1951 sent Joe Louis into a permanent retirement.

Louis's 25 continuous title defences made history as the longest reign for any boxing champion in any weight class. The impact of Joe's achievements went beyond boxing. His rivalry with Schmeling passed through the period of the Second World War. It united America behind an African American boxer against the Nazi regime.

Across his career Louis used his powerful left jab and right hand to defeat many named opponents. The likes of Buddy Baer, Billy Conn, Tommy Farr and Jack Sharkey are all on his record.

A keen all-round sportsman, Louis enjoyed golf and organised tournaments while campaigning for equality within the game. In 1943 he appeared alongside future US president Ronald Reagan in an army film. Louis struggled with personal problems throughout his life and died in 1981.

RAY ROBINSON

Nicknames	Sugar Ray
Nationality	American
Weight(s)	Lightweight, Welterweight, Middleweight, Light heavyweight
Height	1.80 m (5 ft 11 in)
Stance	Orthodox

FIRST FIGHT 1940

RETIRED 1965

TOTAL FIGHTS	201

WINS	WINS BY KO	LOSSES	DRAWS
174	109	19	6

BIOGRAPHY

Sugar Ray Robinson was born as Walker Smith Jr on the 3rd of May 1921 in Ailey, Georgia. As a teenager Walker wanted to enter an amateur tournament but was too young. He borrowed a birth certificate from a friend named Ray Robinson, and a boxing legend was born.

His exact amateur record is sketchy as Robinson boxed under different names, but he was a big puncher who lost very few contests once he reached a high level. Sugar Ray won double gold at the New York Golden Gloves and two gold medals at the Intercity Golden Gloves.

Turning professional in 1940 Ray made a winning start with a second-round KO. In this era the likes of Robinson would box many non-title fights despite being a world champion.

Across his long career Robinson had many rivalries. One of his most frequent opponents was Jake LaMotta, who later had a film made about him called Raging Bull. Robinson fought LaMotta six times and beat him on five of those occasions. Robinson also boxed Carl 'Bobo' Olson four times. Olson was from Hawaii and later became the middleweight champion, but he could never beat Robinson.

Robinson defeated the great Henry Armstrong in 1943, although Armstrong was past his best at this stage. Early in his career Robinson beat Fritzie Zivic twice, both times in New York. Zivic had previously been the world welterweight champion.

Sugar Ray had four tough fights with Gene Fullmer who was

the world middleweight champion. He also fought Carmen Basilio who retired as a welterweight and middleweight world champion. Robinson twice beat Kid Gavilan aka 'The Cuban Hawk'.

In 1951, Robinson travelled to London to fight Randolph 'Randy' Turpin. The fighter from Leamington Spa was a good boxer but not expected to defeat such a top champion. Turpin fought the fight of his life and defeated Robinson over 15 rounds. Robinson won the rematch by knockout, but he was starting to decline. Even so, Ray knocked out Rocky Graziano, who was a former middleweight world champion and one of boxing's hardest punchers.

Robinson was inducted into the International Boxing Hall of Fame in 1990. He is regarded by many fight historians as the greatest boxer of all time and held the world title at welterweight and middleweight. Robinson had excellent foot movement that allowed him to move around an opponent and let go with his fast-handed combinations. His jab to the head and body was strong. He finished or hurt many opponents with his right uppercut.

Overall, he took part in 201 recorded fights, scoring 174 wins, with 109 knockouts. Robinson lost 19 times overall but only once was he stopped. That was a 13th-round retirement loss to Joey Maxim in 1952 when they fought in such heat that the referee collapsed.

Robinson was a very good singer and dancer who also played the trumpet. He drove a bright pink Cadillac car and had many people travel with him when he fought in different countries, including a personal barber.

TRAF

THOMAS HEARNS

Nicknames	Hitman, Motor City Cobra
Nationality	American
Weight(s)	Welterweight, Light middleweight, Middleweight, Super middleweight, Light heavyweight, Cruiserweight
Height	1.85 m (6 ft 1 in)
Stance	Orthodox

FIRST FIGHT 1977

RETIRED 2006

TOTAL FIGHTS	67

WINS	WINS BY KO	LOSSES	DRAWS
61	48	5	1

BIOGRAPHY

Thomas Hearns was born on the 18th of October 1958 in Grand Junction, Tennessee. Young Tommy had a tough upbringing as his mother struggled to raise him and his eight brothers and sisters. After the family moved to Detroit, Hearns began amateur boxing and won titles. His best moment came in 1977 when he won the National Golden Gloves at light-welterweight.

Once in Detroit, Hearns hooked up with legendary trainer Emanuel Steward of the Kronk Gym. Steward helped train Hearns to be a devastating puncher and he knocked out his first 17 professional opponents. In 1979 Alfonso Hayman took Hearns 10 rounds. It was the first time he had gone the distance.

Keeping very busy, fighting regularly every few months, Hearns eventually got his first world title opportunity in 1980 against WBA welterweight champion Pipino Cuevas. Cuevas was making the 12th defence of his title, but Hearns blew him away in two rounds.

Hearns made three defences of the belt before he unified in 1981 against WBC welterweight champion Sugar Ray Leonard. It was a fantastic fight between two prime warriors. Leonard eventually knocked out Hearns in round 14 of a 15-round contest. It was voted as Ring Magazine Fight of the Year.

Hearns moved up in weight and bounced back in 1982 by winning the WBC title at super-welterweight with a points win over a great fighter called Wilfred Benitez.

In 1984 Hearns defended the title in Las Vegas against Roberto Duran. In round two Hearns landed one of the great one-punch KO finishes that knocked Duran out cold.

Hearns then moved up to middleweight and in 1985 fought Marvin Hagler for all three of the belts at 160 pounds. Hearns was knocked out in round three of an extreme war. The phrase "having a Hagler-Hearns" has since been used in boxing to describe an exciting fight.

Tall and rangy at 6'1", with a 78" reach, Hearns climbed up in weight. He knocked out Britain's Dennis Andries at light-heavyweight before moving back down to middleweight to fight Iran Barkley.

In 1989 Hearns fought a rematch with old opponent Sugar Ray Leonard. Hearns dropped Leonard twice, but the fight ended in a draw decision. Hearns boxed until 2006 and ended up competing as a cruiserweight. He fought in Manchester, England in 1999 on a Prince Naseem Hamed undercard.

Hearns finished up with 48 KOs from 61 wins and was a ferocious finisher with massive punching power, good boxing skills and a powerful jab. Another of his nicknames was 'The Motor City Cobra' named after his links to Detroit. He faced six undefeated fighters across a 29-year career and beat them all. Hearns ended up winning world titles in five weight divisions. He boxed as low as 144 pounds and as high as 191 pounds as his lean physique carried the extra weight.

Tommy's mother, Lois Hearns, was a fight promoter on the Detroit scene. Nicknamed 'The Chosen One', his son Ronald Hearns boxed for 11 years, ending with 28 wins.

ROCKY MARCIANO

Nicknames	The Brockton Blockbuster
Nationality	American
Weight(s)	Heavyweight
Height	1.78 m (5 ft 10 in)
Stance	Orthodox

FIRST FIGHT 1947

RETIRED 1955

TOTAL FIGHTS	49

WINS	WINS BY KO	LOSSES	DRAWS
49	43	0	0

BIOGRAPHY

Rocky Marciano was born as Rocco Francis Marchegiano on the 1st of September 1923 in Brockton, Massachusetts. A naturally strong man, Marciano enjoyed weightlifting as a youngster. His amateur career never took off as he was drafted into the United States army.

Turning professional in 1947, the Brockton brawler briefly went back to the amateurs before turning over for real in 1948. Rocky raced to 16-0, all by knockout, before Don Mogard became the first man to take him the distance. Even at this early stage some opponents were able to win rounds and display better boxing skills than 'Rocco Marchegiano' but the man who would soon become Rocky Marciano had the desire and power to defeat anyone.

On his way to a world title shot, Marciano battled past two tough Bronx boxers in Carmine 'Bingo' Vingo, who he knocked out, and unbeaten Roland LaStarza who he outlasted on a split decision. The LaStarza fight was very closely contested, but Rocky got the nod.

He moved on to add the recognised name of former champion Joe Louis to his record by eighth-round stoppage in 1951 and the following year defeated 89-fight veteran Harry Matthews in a world title eliminator.

When he finally fought the champion, Jersey Joe Walcott, Marciano was dropped in round one by a left hook. The challenger was struggling badly with a broken nose and behind on the scorecards when he finally turned it around.

Rocky landed his 'Suzie Q' right hand to knock the older man out in round 13.

They fought a rematch in 1953 and Marciano took Walcott out in round one to properly begin his successful title run. The first defence was a knockout win over old foe Roland LaStarza before a difficult points win over Ezzard Charles. Marciano then knocked the former heavyweight king out in round eight of their rematch.

Rocky closed his career out with a KO of London's Don Cockell and a stoppage of Archie Moore. The 'Old Mongoose' floored Marciano early but was on the end of a beating for much of the bout. Rocky decided to leave the sport on his own terms and the win over Moore in 1955 was his final bout.

Short for a heavyweight of modern standards, Marciano made up for his size with ferocious punching power, good stamina, relentless will to win and a solid chin that could absorb heavy blows.

Marciano's heavyweight title reign was filled with explosive knockouts. Only Ezzard Charles managed to last the 15-round distance and Marciano stopped him in their rematch. Rocky held the heavyweight world championship for four years and placed his name in the history books as the only heavyweight champion to retire undefeated.

As a baby, Marciano contracted pneumonia and almost died. Long before his boxing career he held a variety of manual labour jobs. Marciano worked as a ditch digger, shoemaker and coal supplier.

TRAI

ROY JONES JR

Nicknames	Captain Hook, Superman, RJ
Nationality	American and Russian
Weight(s)	Middleweight, Super middleweight, Light heavyweight, Cruiserweight, Heavyweight
Height	1.80 m (5 ft 11 in)
Stance	Orthodox

FIRST FIGHT
1989

RETIRED
2018

TOTAL FIGHTS	75

WINS	WINS BY KO	LOSSES	DRAWS
66	47	9	0

BIOGRAPHY

Roy Levesta Jones Jr was born on the 16th of January 1969 in Pensacola, Florida. His father, Roy Jones Sr, was a disciplinarian who had fought in the Vietnam War. Jones Sr boxed as a middleweight in the 1970s but ended his short career on a losing streak.

He took control of his son's prospects early on and young Roy excelled as an amateur, winning the Golden Gloves and a gold medal in the 1984 US National Junior Olympics. The Olympics would later cause Jones Jr heartbreak as he lost in the final of the 1988 Seoul Games in what was described as one of the worst decisions of all time.

Turning professional in 1989 Jones raced to 21-0 with 20 KOs before securing a vacant IBF middleweight title shot in 1993 against future great Bernard Hopkins. Jones beat Hopkins on points, and soon went on to defeat another great fighter, James Toney, on points. That was in 1994 as Jones moved up to super-middleweight.

In 1997, Jones controversially lost for the first time when he was disqualified in round nine for hitting Montell Griffin while Griffin was down. After defeating Griffin by a stunning first-round knockout in their rematch, from 1998-2004 Jones was a virtually untouchable star of boxing. By this point he was a world champion at light-heavyweight and gathered up a handful of titles.

During this time Jones defeated Australia's Glen Kelly by putting his hands behind his back and knocking out Kelly as he tried to attack. In 2003 Jones made history by moving up to heavyweight to defeat the much bigger John Ruiz for a world title.

This was the best version of Jones fans would ever see. He quickly moved back down to light-heavyweight but struggled to defeat Antonio Tarver on points, before Tarver stunningly knocked him out in a rematch. Jones was stopped soon after by Glen Johnson and the decline had set in.

He ended up fighting for lesser titles, against strange opponents, including fighters who had been voted for by the public. He boxed in Latvia, Poland, Australia and Russia, even becoming an official Russian citizen.

While Jones is considered to have gone on past his prime, the Florida boxer is still recognised as one of the greatest boxers not only of his generation but of all time. He held many belts in four weight classes, including undisputed status and was voted Fighter of the Decade by the Boxing Writers' Association.

At his best, Jones had very fast hands, athletic ability and moved in unpredictable ways.

For decades Roy lived on a farm in Florida. Jones was criticised for being involved in rooster fighting tournaments and he was accused of animal cruelty

On the morning of his world title fight with Eric Lucas in 1996, Jones played in a professional basketball match, becoming the only athlete to compete in two paid sports on the same day. Roy has also released rap albums and would often enter the ring singing his own songs.

HENRY ARMSTRONG

Nicknames	Homicide Hank
Nationality	American
Weight(s)	Featherweight, Lightweight, Welterweight, Middleweight
Height	1.66 m (5 ft 5½ in)
Stance	Orthodox

RETIRED
1945

FIRST
FIGHT
1931

TOTAL FIGHTS	181

WINS	WINS BY KO	LOSSES	DRAWS
151	101	21	9

BIOGRAPHY

Known during his career as Henry Armstrong, Henry Jackson Jr was born on the 12th of December 1912 in Columbus, Mississippi. Armstrong was raised during a period of great prejudice. His father, Henry Jackson Sr, was a sharecropper and the family migrated north which eventually led Henry Jr into a boxing club.

Armstrong based himself in Los Angeles with an eye on Olympic qualification but despite a strong amateur career that ran from 1929 to 1932, he failed to qualify for the 1932 Games and instead turned professional.

The fights, wins, draws and losses came quickly as Armstrong learned his trade the hard way. By the time he faced Petey Sarron for the featherweight world title it was towards the end of a whirlwind 1937. Armstrong won by sixth-round KO and was named as the Ring Magazine Fighter of the Year for 1937 as he took part in 27 contests, winning them all, with 26 by knockout.

In May 1938 he widely outpointed the excellent Barney Ross to win world honours at welterweight. Just three months later he slimmed back down to lightweight to defend his title by split decision over New York's 'Herkimer Hurricane' Lou Ambers. Three months after that he was back up at welterweight defeating Filipino native Ceferino Garcia across the 15-round stretch.

Moving through the weight classes, in 1939 Armstrong defeated Lew Feldman with both the lightweight and welterweight titles on the line. Armstrong lost twice to Fritzie

Zivic as his momentum slowed and a decade of hard fights took their toll. In 1943 a faded Armstrong was carried for 10 rounds by an up-and-coming force of world boxing named Sugar Ray Robinson.

Armstrong is recognised as one of the greatest fighters of all time. He held the featherweight, lightweight and welterweight world titles back when there was only one champion, and it was becoming more difficult to avoid fighters of any ethnicity. Remarkably, at one point he held those three world championships all at the same time.

Celebrated boxing historian Bert Sugar rated Armstrong as the second-best boxer of all time. He regularly appears in the top five all-time pound-for-pound lists and was inducted into the International Boxing Hall of Fame in 1990, two years after his death.

A welterweight legend, Armstrong successfully defended his title at 147 pounds on 19 occasions. Overall, he took part in 1155 rounds across 180 bouts, with 149 wins.

Sometimes nicknamed 'Hammerin' Hank' or 'Hurricane Hank' Armstrong's style was relentless. He applied non-stop pressure to his opponents, who would need to be in top physical shape to compete with his pace. Armstrong swarmed anyone he faced from the first round, rolling shoulder to shoulder, fighting on the inside.

Away from the ropes Armstong was a quiet man who engaged in religious work after retiring. He was an ordained Baptist minister who helped mentor young people who had taken a wrong path in life. Henry also owned a nightclub called Melody Room which referenced his early career name of Melody Jackson.

TRAF

JULIO CESAR CHAVEZ

Nicknames	JC, Superstar, Mr. KO
Nationality	Mexican
Weight(s)	Super featherweight, Lightweight, Light welterweight, Welterweight
Height	1.71 m (5 ft 7½ in)
Stance	Orthodox

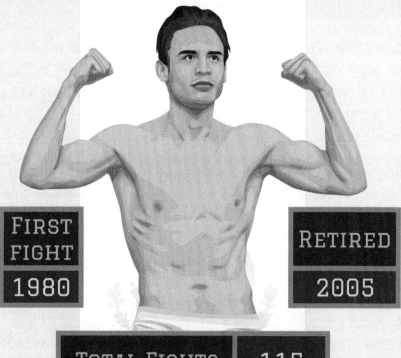

FIRST FIGHT
1980

RETIRED
2005

TOTAL FIGHTS	115

WINS	WINS BY KO	LOSSES	DRAWS
107	86	6	2

BIOGRAPHY

Julio Cesar Chavez Gonzalez was born on the 12th of July 1962 in Obregon, Mexico. As part of a large family Chavez grew up extremely poor and turned to boxing to provide a better life for his mother who worked hard doing domestic jobs.

After working on his skills as an amateur, Chavez moved to Tijuana to box as a professional, earning money. His first fight came in 1980 aged 17. Chavez fought a string of debutants early on, mostly in Sinaloa, and was soon boxing 10-round fights.

His first big title opportunity came in 1984 when he defeated fellow-Mexican Mario Martinez to win the vacant WBC super-featherweight. After this victory Chavez never looked back. He made several successful defences, beating good opponents like Rocky Lockridge, Juan Laporte and Roger Mayweather who he knocked out in two rounds. Chavez moved up to lightweight and knocked out quality Puerto Rican Edwin 'Chapo' Rosario to become a two-division champion.

His stay at 135 pounds was short lived as he moved up to challenge old foe Roger Mayweather for 'Black Mamba's' WBC super-lightweight title. Chavez won by retirement in round 10 but his lengthy run of defences was close to coming to a premature end in 1990 when he won a controversial bout against Meldrick Taylor. Chavez was losing on the cards when the referee jumped in with only seconds to go and stop Taylor on his feet.

In 1993 over 132,000 fans packed into the Azteca Stadium to witness their hero knock out Greg Haugen in five rounds. Later that year Chavez moved up briefly to challenge Pernell Whitaker at welterweight. Julio received a draw in a fight he seemed to have lost. Chavez did indeed lose for the first time in 1994 when Frankie Randall defeated him in Las Vegas.

Chavez fought on for a further nine years, losing twice to an up-and-coming Oscar De La Hoya and suffering a knockout loss to Kostya Tszyu for his old WBC super-lightweight title. Chavez lost on his final ever pro appearance in 2005. He took part in 115 contests overall.

Chavez boxed professionally for 25 years in total, and he won world titles in three weight classes. He won Fighter of the Year honours and pound-for-pound recognition from both the Ring Magazine and Boxing Writers of America.

He made nine defences of the WBC super-featherweight title, two defences of his WBA lightweight belt and 16 total defences of his super-lightweight strap. In 2010 Chavez was inducted into the International Boxing Hall of Fame.

Chavez was an aggressive fighter with a lot of technical ability. He pressured opponents to head and body, closing the distance and attacking the body with his left hook.

Julio took on commentary work for Mexican TV after retiring. He once featured in ESPN's top 50 fighters of all-time countdown. Two of Chavez's sons took after their father and entered the ring. Julio Junior won the WBC middleweight title in 2011 while Omar was a hard-punching super-welterweight contender.

JOE CALZAGHE

Nicknames	Pride of Wales
Nationality	Welsh
Weight(s)	Super-middleweight, Light-heavyweight
Height	1.83 m (6 ft 0 in)
Stance	Southpaw

FIRST FIGHT

1993

RETIRED

2008

TOTAL FIGHTS	46

WINS	WINS BY KO	LOSSES	DRAWS
46	32	0	0

BIOGRAPHY

Joseph William Calzaghe was born on the 23rd of March 1972 in Hammersmith, London. Calzaghe has an Italian background and grew up in Wales. A keen footballer, Joe joined Newbridge Boxing Club at the age of 10 and as his talent developed he switched his focus fully on to boxing.

Across his 15-year career Joe was trained by his father Enzo Calzaghe. Enzo was a musician who had no formal training in the art of boxing yet became one of the UK's most respected and successful coaches.

After winning Schoolboy titles Calzaghe moved up to Senior level and won the ABAs three years in a row, from 1990-1993, rising in weight each time as his body developed. Signing with promoter Frank Warren, Calzaghe turned professional in 1993. He could not have asked for a bigger stage. His debut was on the undercard of Lennox Lewis vs. Frank Bruno in Cardiff.

Calzaghe won the British title in 1996 and made one defence before winning the world title in 1997 by beating Chris Eubank over 12 rounds. Calzaghe went on a long run of defences that included wins over the likes of Robin Reid, Richie Woodhall, Charles Brewer, Byron Mitchell and two knockouts of Mario Veit.

One of the greatest tests of Calzaghe's career came in 2006 when he faced IBF champion Jeff Lacy. The fight took place in Manchester, UK but was shown in the early hours of the morning for American television. Lacy was an undefeated, big puncher and many thought he would be too strong.

Calzaghe dominated the fight from start to finish with his speed and boxing ability.

In 2007, Calzaghe beat another undefeated champion in Mikkel Kessler. Coming from Denmark, Kessler had the two remaining belts that Calzaghe had not yet claimed. Joe won on points in front of his home fans.

Coming to the end of his career, Calzaghe moved up in weight to fight twice in America. He first defeated Bernard Hopkins in Las Vegas and then Roy Jones Jr in New York. Calzaghe was put on the floor in the first round of both contests yet came back to win on points.

Overall, Calzaghe made 21 defences of his WBO super-middleweight title and unified the other belts at various times. His two fights at light-heavyweight had no titles on the line but were against legendary names.

As he got older, Calzaghe had hand problems that occasionally stopped fights from happening and threatened to end his career. Even though he was dropped by lesser opponents, Joe had a solid chin and great powers of recovery.

Joe formed Calzaghe Promotions alongside his father, but it did not last long. Calzaghe is a big football fan and supports Juventus. He is also a big fan of red meat and credits his diet with maintaining strength. He also had a fear of flying.

Calzaghe later promoted anti-bullying campaigns as he was picked on at school himself. He has also taken part in celebrity football tournaments since his retirement.

TRAI

GEORGE FOREMAN

Nicknames	Big George
Nationality	American
Weight(s)	Heavyweight
Height	1.91 m (6 ft 3 in)
Stance	Orthodox

FIRST FIGHT
1969

RETIRED
1997

TOTAL FIGHTS	81

WINS	WINS BY KO	LOSSES	DRAWS
76	68	5	0

BIOGRAPHY

George Edward Foreman was born on the 10th of January 1949 in Marshall, Texas. Foreman's physique always suited the fight game and he excelled as an amateur boxer, winning a gold medal in the 1968 Olympic Games in Mexico City.

Foreman's amateur stint was short yet successful and his heavy hands clearly suited the professional game. Turning pro in 1969 Foreman started as he meant to go on - by delivering a crushing knockout.

In 1973, Foreman displayed next-level power when he battered Joe Frazier in two rounds to become the WBA and WBC heavyweight champion. Another two-round blitz of Ken Norton in 1974 reinforced his brute strength.

Never one to refuse a challenge, in 1974 Muhammad Ali adopted a rope-a-dope strategy and outlasted Foreman over eight rounds in Kinshasa. The fight was tagged 'The Rumble in the Jungle' and is an iconic clash of boxing stars.

When Foreman was outpointed by Jimmy Young in 1977 he hung up the gloves and many thought it was the last time we would see him in action.

This would not be the case as 10 years later he returned to the ring. Foreman's career is split into two sections, and he is responsible for one of boxing's biggest comebacks. Not only due to his age but also in the fight itself against Michael Moorer.

After stringing together a run of wins over varying levels of opposition, Foreman lost a competitive challenge to Evander

Holyfield in Atlantic City in 1991. Still feeling as if he had something to offer, George fought on and 17 months after losing to Tommy Morrison he got a shot at Michael Moorer who had since defeated Holyfield. Foreman was outboxed by the southpaw for most of the contest, but he kept the faith and landed a knockout right hand in round 10 to cause a stunning upset. Foreman became a world champion again, regaining the title he had lost 20 years earlier to Ali.

Always known for his chilling punch power, Foreman's style changed in his second career run. He conserved energy more, relying on his strong jab and right-hand equaliser, making sure he did not gas out given added weight.

George often features in the top 10 greatest heavyweight lists and is one of boxing's biggest ever punchers. Foreman's career spanned 28 years and the Texan took part in 81 bouts, winning 76 with 68 by KO. He lost five times and Muhammad Ali was the only man to stop him.

After his second retirement Foreman operated as a ringside analyst on HBO boxing. He famously kept his colleagues safe during a riot after the Riddick Bowe vs. Andrew Golota contest.

A big fan of barbecue, Foreman attached his name to the George Foreman grill. It is reported that he made more money from the sales of the grills than from his long boxing career.

Foreman has seven daughters and five sons. All his sons are named George. Foreman is an ordained minister who became a Christian during his career.

BERNARD HOPKINS

Nicknames	The Executioner, The Alien
Nationality	American
Weight(s)	Middleweight, Light heavyweight
Height	1.85 m (6 ft 1 in)
Stance	Orthodox

FIRST FIGHT

1988

RETIRED

2016

TOTAL FIGHTS	67

WINS	WINS BY KO	LOSSES	DRAWS
55	32	8	2

BIOGRAPHY

Bernard Humphrey Hopkins Jr was born on the 15th of January 1965 in Philadelphia. Hopkins is noted as a success story in both boxing and life. Growing up on the streets of Philadelphia, Hopkins soon fell into a life of crime and received a long prison sentence at 17 years old. Determined to avoid going back to prison Hopkins dedicated himself to boxing.

He had enrolled in the prison's boxing rehabilitation programme so was already familiar with the sport when he got released. Losing his first professional bout in 1988 did not deter Bernard who went on to unsuccessfully box Roy Jones for the world title. Still believing in his abilities, Hopkins drew with Segundo Mercado in Ecuador for the IBF title before winning the rematch by KO.

Hopkins defeated good fighters like Glen Johnson and Robert Allen by knockout as part of a run of defences. He was a strong underdog in 2001 when he defied the odds once again and knocked out unbeaten puncher Felix Trinidad to unify the middleweight titles.

A 2004 knockout of Oscar De La Hoya earned the WBO belt and undisputed status at the weight. After losing twice to Jermain Taylor, Bernard moved up to defeat Antonio Tarver at light-heavyweight.

Every time the ageing maestro seemed ready to retire he would defeat a younger, fresher fighter. Jean Pascal and unbeaten duo Kelly Pavlik and Tavoris Cloud all came unstuck against 'B-Hop' who was still boxing heavy punchers like Sergey Kovalev right up until the end.

This all came from a man who promised his late mother, Shirley Hopkins, that he would retire when he reached 41 years old. Veteran trainer Bouie Fisher and Naazim Richardson were in the corner for many of his biggest nights.

Hopkins is recognised as a modern day great. He made multiple defences of his IBF middleweight title and unified the division. Hopkins boxed for 28 years across 67 bouts. He gathered Ring Magazine, lineal and undisputed honours along the way. He was only stopped once, in his final fight, when Joe Smith Jr knocked him out of the ring.

Hopkins' style changed gradually. Early in his career he would take more chances. As he got older and wiser, he used a more defensive, counter punching style. Bernard liked to slow the pace of fights right down so he could land single shots, especially with the right hand, and win rounds. Never afraid to get dirty and use any method available, Hopkins became a seasoned master of his craft.

Despite having a tough early life, Hopkins turned himself around and was a model professional in the final stages of his career. When he left prison, a warden remarked that he would be seeing him again soon. Hopkins replied that he would never be back in prison, and he never was.

Hopkins later joined up with former victim Oscar De La Hoya, working for Golden Boy Promotions. Bernard also does motivational speeches and has featured as an analyst on fight broadcasts.

TRAI

MIKE TYSON

Nicknames	Iron, Kid Dynamite
Nationality	American
Weight(s)	Heavyweight
Height	1.78 m (5 ft 10 in)
Stance	Orthodox

FIRST FIGHT 1985

RETIRED 2005

TOTAL FIGHTS	58

WINS	WINS BY KO	LOSSES	DRAWS
50	44	6	0

BIOGRAPHY

Michael Gerard Tyson was born on the 30th of June 1966 in Brooklyn, New York. Tyson had a difficult upbringing and found himself mixing with street gangs in high crime areas. Tyson dropped out of school and was discovered by elderly fight figure Cus D'Amato who introduced him to trainer Kevin Rooney.

As an amateur Tyson had success at the National Golden Gloves and Junior Olympics as he worked on his skills and style. However, he never fought at the Olympics after twice losing to future gold medallist Henry Tillman. Tyson later gained his revenge over Tillman as a professional, with a first-round knockout in 1990.

Mike turned pro in 1985 and soon gained a reputation as a fierce finisher, especially in the early rounds of his fights. After 27 wins Tyson challenged Trevor Berbick for the WBC heavyweight title in 1986. Tyson was too ferocious and knocked Berbick out in two rounds to become the youngest ever champion.

After nine defences, including a first-round KO of lineal champion Michael Spinks, Tyson travelled to Japan to defend against James 'Buster' Douglas. Tyson was expected to win with ease, but Douglas pulled off one of the biggest sporting upsets with a round 10 knockout.

Tyson fought Evander Holyfield twice. In their first fight, in 1996, Holyfield knocked Tyson out in round 11. The second bout, in 1997, ended in a bizarre fashion as Tyson bit off part of Holyfield's ear.

Tyson's career was filled with controversial incidents. Not only did he bite Holyfield's ear, but he tried to break Frans Botha's arm and hit Orlin Norris when he was already down. Tyson's fight with Andrew Golota was changed to a no contest. He also missed four years of his career while in prison. Tyson twice fought in the UK in 2000 when he knocked out Julius Francis and Lou Savarese.

A fight between Tyson and rival Lennox Lewis was talked about for years. When they finally fought in 2002 Tyson was not as powerful and Lewis knocked him out in eight rounds. People thought Tyson would find his old magic and have another world title run but he lost his final two fights to opponents he would have knocked when in his prime.

Tyson's punching power, aggressive style and controversial nature made him a fighter worth watching. He generated hundreds of millions of dollars throughout his 20-year career.

'Iron Mike' was also a talented boxer early in his professional life who could duck, move and jab inside. Tyson is in the International Boxing Hall of Fame and a popular media personality and businessman who is known by fight fans of all ages.

A complicated personality, despite his vicious personality Tyson has always kept racing pigeons, often rearing hundreds at a time. He also owned a pet tiger for 16 years.

The heavyweight champion has always been a keen boxing historian and watched thousands of hours of fight tapes as a youngster, gaining a vast knowledge of the greatest fighters of all time.

FLOYD MAYWEATHER JR

Nicknames	Money, Pretty Boy
Nationality	American
Weight(s)	Super featherweight, Lightweight, Light welterweight, Welterweight, Light middleweight
Height	1.73 m (5 ft 8 in)
Stance	Orthodox

FIRST FIGHT 1996

RETIRED 2017

TOTAL FIGHTS	50

WINS	WINS BY KO	LOSSES	DRAWS
50	27	0	0

BIOGRAPHY

Floyd Mayweather was born as Floyd Joy Sinclair on the 24th of February 1977 in Grand Rapids, Michigan. His father, Floyd Sr, and his uncle Roger were also professional boxers. Floyd had a tough childhood, but with boxing in his family he was always likely to pick up the gloves and start prize fighting. Floyd excelled as an amateur and won National tournaments before qualifying for the 1996 Olympic Games at featherweight.

He won three bouts before being eliminated in the semi-finals by a Bulgarian fighter. The decision was controversial but an official protest by the American team was unsuccessful.

Mayweather moved on and turned professional, making his debut in 1996 in Las Vegas. Mayweather coasted through many of his early fights and his speed and skills made boxing fans take notice.

Mayweather won the WBC super-featherweight title in 1998 when the champion Genaro Hernandez retired after eight rounds. Floyd went on to make nine defences of that title. The most impressive was a 2001 stoppage of unbeaten Diego Corrales.

When Floyd moved up to lightweight in 2002, he had one of the toughest fights of his entire career, against Jose Luis Castillo. Many believed Castillo beat him, but Floyd came back to convincingly win a rematch.

Mayweather gradually moved through the weight classes as he got older. He won many world titles at super-lightweight, welterweight and super-welterweight while beating top boxing names.

2007 was a breakout year as Floyd first beat Oscar De La Hoya who was a recognisable Pay-Per-View star of American boxing. Later in that year he defeated UK fighter Ricky Hatton in Las Vegas. Shortly after fighting Hatton, he announced his retirement and did not box again for two years, when he returned to beat Juan Manuel Marquez.

Mayweather was hurt early in his 2010 fight with Shane Mosley but came back to win strongly. In 2013 he beat Saul 'Canelo' Alvarez who would go on to become a dominant force in boxing.

Marcos Maidana gave Mayweather two hard fights in 2014 as the champion came towards the end of his career. Floyd defeated MMA star Conor McGregor in his final ever legitimate contest, in 2017.

The highest Mayweather ever weighed was 151 pounds against Miguel Cotto in 2012. The one-sided beating of Arturo Gatti in 2005 was one of his most complete performances.

Later in his career Floyd became known as one of the greatest defensive boxers of all time. However, early on he was a spiteful finisher who could drop opponents with fast shots. He suffered from hand problems and changed his style to protect his knuckles. In total, Floyd won 15 world championships, including lineal and undisputed status in some weight classes.

In 2008 Floyd made a surprise appearance at Wrestle mania, taking on the gigantic 'Big Show' character. Known for his outrageous wealth and love of money, Floyd has a generous side. In 2011 he paid for the funeral of former opponent Genaro Hernandez, and he has made numerous charitable donations to hospitals and hospices.

MARVIN HAGLER

Nicknames	Marvelous
Nationality	American
Weight(s)	Middleweight
Height	1.75 m (5 ft 9 in)
Stance	Southpaw

FIRST FIGHT 1973

RETIRED 1987

TOTAL FIGHTS	67

WINS	WINS BY KO	LOSSES	DRAWS
62	52	3	2

BIOGRAPHY

Marvin Nathaniel Hagler was born on the 23rd of May 1954 in Newark, New Jersey. Despite being raised by his mother in New Jersey, Hagler and his family moved to Brockton, Massachusetts to escape riots that were happening in their area.

Hagler hooked up with boxing trainer Goody Petronelli and his brother Pat. Marvin would stick with the brothers as his trainer and manager throughout his amateur and professional career. Hagler lied about his age so he could be allowed to box in amateur tournaments. He grew into a strong fighter and won the 1973 US National Championships at middleweight.

He turned pro later that year and across his 14 years always boxed around 160 pounds. After some early career setbacks, including two losses and a draw, Hagler finally got his shot at the WBC and WBA middleweight titles in 1979 when he fought Italy's Vito Antuofermo. Even though it seemed like Hagler had won the fight, it was declared a draw and Hagler waited patiently for another shot.

In 1980 Antuofermo had lost the belts to Alan Minter, so Hagler travelled to the UK to cut Minter so badly that he was stopped after three rounds. There were 12,000 people at the fight and the British fans were so angry that they threw bottles and cups at the new champion as he left the ring.

Hagler returned to the United States and went on a run of defences. This included a revenge victory over Vito Antuofermo, a first-round KO win over hard-hitting William

'Caveman' Lee and a win over Britain's Tony Sibson. Hagler also picked up the IBF middleweight title by knocking out Wilford Scypion.

Hagler beat Roberto Duran on points and knocked out Thomas Hearns in a rollercoaster three-round fight in 1985. While Hagler was beating undefeated John 'The Beast' Mugabi in 1986, Sugar Ray Leonard was watching at ringside. Even though he was officially retired, Leonard suddenly decided that he could beat Hagler. He challenged the champion, who accepted, and they faced off in Las Vegas, 1987. Leonard won a disputed decision and Marvin was so angry that he never fought again.

Hagler was an outstanding fighter and champion. From 1980 to 1987 he reigned as the undisputed middleweight king, making 12 defences against top contenders. Only Roberto Duran managed to last the 15-round distance in this time. All other 11 opponents were stopped.

Hagler was inducted into the International Boxing Hall of Fame and regularly appears in greatest fighter pound-for-pound lists. Not only was he a massive puncher, with a 78 percent KO ratio, but was only officially knocked down once and was never knocked out. Hagler was a southpaw who watched his opponents' early movements while bobbing and weaving, behind a solid jab.

After his loss to Sugar Ray Leonard, Hagler moved to Italy and lived a quiet life with his second wife. He starred in several movies, including a role in the action thriller Indio. Hagler died in 2021, aged 66, while back in America.

RAY LEONARD

Nicknames	Sugar
Nationality	American
Weight(s)	Welterweight, Light middleweight, Middleweight, Super middleweight, Light heavyweight
Height	1.75 m (5 ft 9 in)
Stance	Orthodox

FIRST FIGHT
1977

RETIRED
1997

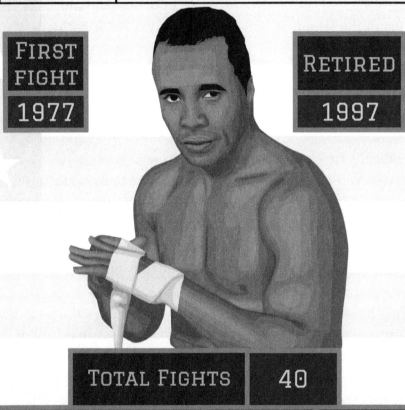

TOTAL FIGHTS	40

WINS	WINS BY KO	LOSSES	DRAWS
36	25	3	1

BIOGRAPHY

Ray Charles Leonard was born on the 17th of May 1956 in Wilmington, North Carolina. Unlike many boxers, Leonard did not have a troubled childhood. While he was a good student and not drawn to the streets, he was still tough and competitive, especially in sports.

Ray followed his older brother into boxing and was an outstanding amateur, winning the Nation Golden Gloves, Pan American Games and numerous other medals. His finest achievement was a gold medal at the 1976 Olympic Games where he swept past every opponent he faced, without dropping a round.

Leonard's first major professional glory came in 1979 when he knocked out Wilfred Benitez in round 15 to win the WBC welterweight title. Two fights later Leonard was beaten on points by the legendary Roberto Duran. He rebounded strongly from that first loss by outboxing Duran in a rematch so much that the Panamanian refused to continue fighting.

After a close first bout Leonard and his team used a strategy of movement and taunting to throw Duran off his rhythm. It worked. Even though the fight was close, Leonard annoyed Duran who said "No Mas" or "No More" in Spanish and called it a night. Leonard later defeated Duran in a third fight when both men were past their best.

In their 1981 Fight of the Year Ray inflicted the first career defeat on Thomas 'Hitman' Hearns with a 14th-round KO win. They fought again in 1989 and it ended in a draw. Leonard came out of retirement to defeat Marvin Hagler in 1987. It was the first time Hagler had lost in 11 years and the Brockton boxer never fought again.

When Leonard defeated Donny Lalonde in 1988, he made history by winning the WBC title at both super-middleweight and light-heavyweight. Ray also snapped the 36-0 record of dangerous Ugandan southpaw Ayub Kalule when they fought in 1981.

Leonard won world titles in five weight classes across 20 years as a professional fighter and was a lineal champion (the man who beat the man) at three of those weights. He was named as the Boxer of the Decade for the 1980s and was the first fighter to earn over $100 million in purses.

With his shining smile and likeable personality, Leonard filled a gap created by the decline of Muhammad Ali. His part in the 'Four Kings' era, alongside Hagler, Hearns and Duran, helped keep boxing exciting and relevant. Leonard was trained by Muhammad Ali's old coach Angelo Dundee.

At his peak Leonard was a very talented fighter with fast hands, great balance and movement. His strong jab made openings for the overhand right and left hook. Despite his ability he was never afraid to mix it up with tough guys either.

Following retirement Leonard was seen regularly as a boxing pundit and television analyst. He set-up his own promotional company and starred on reality TV. As such a popular personality Leonard has also appeared in films, provided motivational speeches and featured on advertisements.

TRAI

ROBERTO DURAN

Nicknames	El Cholo, Manos de Piedra
Nationality	Panamanian
Weight(s)	Super featherweight, Lightweight, Light welterweight, Welterweight, Light middleweight, Middleweight, Super middleweight
Height	1.70 m (5 ft 7 in)
Stance	Orthodox

FIRST FIGHT
1970

RETIRED
2001

TOTAL FIGHTS	119

WINS	WINS BY KO	LOSSES	DRAWS
103	70	16	0

BIOGRAPHY

Roberto Duran Samaniego was born on the 16th of June 1961 in El Chorrillo, Panama. Duran first laced up the gloves at an early age and was sparring experienced opponents from eight years old. Life was difficult and he had to fight his way out of a tough neighbourhood.

Finishing early with an amateur career that barely touched 30 contests, Duran turned professional in 1968 aged 16. Fighting was in his nature and Duran recorded some impressive knockouts in Panama City. As the level of opposition rose, KO wins over the likes of Ernesto Marcel and Japanese veteran Hiroshi Kobayashi earned him a shot at WBA lightweight champion Ken Buchanan in 1972.

Duran mauled and brawled the Scotsman to a round 13 defeat and claimed his first world crown. Despite losing in a non-title bout to Esteban De Jesus, three fights later, Duran went on a long run of defences that included two revenge knockout wins over De Jesus.

Duran fought Sugar Ray Leonard three times in total. The first two meetings came in 1980 at welterweight. Duran handed Leonard his first career loss in their first fight before Leonard won the rematch when Duran bailed out in round eight. Leonard dominated their third meeting in 1989 when the pair were at super-middleweight and getting older.

Other notable names on the Duran resume include Edwin Viruet, Carlos Palomino, Davey Moore and Iran Barkley. 'The Blade' was a big, strong middleweight and Duran rolled back the clock to deliver his last great performance to claim victory over Barkley.

Duran also mixed with Marvin Hagler (lost on points) and Thomas Hearns (stopped brutally in two rounds). By this point he was still competing with the best but way beyond his natural weight class. As his career ended, he was still smart enough to survive against the likes of Hector Camacho and Vinny Pazienza twice.

Duran's remarkable run as a professional boxer lasted 33 years in total, across 119 contests. Winning world titles at four different weight classes, the Panamanian also claimed undisputed and lineal statuses along the way. Overall, he won 103 bouts and knocked out 70 opponents.

Duran's career spanned five decades, and he retired many times, although his final retirement came at the age of 50. Some observers consider Duran to be the greatest lightweight of all time.

Duran was a versatile boxer who was able to pull several tricks in the ring. He could step off and box when required but mostly his hard-punching pressure and inside fighting made him a top-level fighter. Duran was able to duck, weave and roll on the inside, slicing hooks and uppercuts to the head and body, making it very difficult to defend against his attacks.

Active outside of the ring, Duran once released a Salsa music album and is a licensed aircraft pilot. Roberto's daughter followed in his footsteps and boxed without any great success. Duran was inducted into the official Boxing Hall of Fame in 2007.

ANDRE WARD

Nicknames	Son of God
Nationality	American
Weight(s)	Super middleweight, Light heavyweight
Height	1.83 m (6 ft 0 in)
Stance	Orthodox

FIRST FIGHT 2004

RETIRED 2017

TOTAL FIGHTS	32

WINS	WINS BY KO	LOSSES	DRAWS
32	16	0	0

BIOGRAPHY

Andre Michael Ward was born on the 23rd of February 1984 in Oakland, California. He first started boxing at the age of nine when his father took him to a gym. Ward's parents had issues and trainer Virgil Hunter took a strong interest in Ward's life and boxing development.

Starting off as a middleweight, Ward won US National Championships as an amateur and qualified for the 2004 Olympics in Athens. By this time Ward had filled out to light-heavyweight and he fought hard to win the gold medal.

Ward turned professional in 2004 at super-middleweight. As a gold medallist he was closely watched by many of the top promoters. Most of Ward's early fights were in the United States, but he also fought in the Cayman Islands and St Lucia. For long spells of his career, Ward headlined in his native Oakland.

As his record improved, unbeaten Ward became a showcase attraction fighter on powerful television station Showtime. With his record at 20-0 Ward entered the inaugural super-six tournament but was not regarded as one of the favourites.

He defied the odds. In his first fight Ward became a world champion by defeating Mikkel Kessler, the joint tournament favourite, as Kessler suffered with bad cuts from head clashes. Throughout his career Ward was accused of using head butts and various other rough tactics to win.

He defeated Allan Green to progress further through the super-six and then beat long-reigning world champion

Arthur Abraham from Germany. This set up a final against Carl Froch from the UK.

Ward won the entire competition by defeating Froch on points in Atlantic City, while taking Froch's title to become a unified world champion. Andre defended the titles against reigning light-heavyweight champion Chad Dawson who moved down a division for the opportunity to burst Ward's bubble. Dawson struggled badly with the weight and was dropped multiple times before being knocked out.

After a long time out of the ring Ward moved himself up to light-heavyweight. Injuries and inactivity were taking their toll as he struggled to look impressive against lesser opponents. He still retained a steely resolve to be the best.

His final two fights came against the same opponent. Russia's Sergey Kovalev was a feared puncher who had never been beaten. In what was the toughest test of his career Ward was dropped in the second round by Kovalev. He battled back to win by a point on all three judges' scorecards which were totalled at 114-113.

Many fans and ringside observers thought Kovalev won the fight, so they had a rematch. Ward knocked Kovalev out in round eight and announced shortly after that he would retire, undefeated.

Ward is a Christian who often travels to schools and youth centres to offer positive messages and motivational talks. Unlike many great boxing champions, he quit the sport in good health and resisted the temptation to return. The Californian later appeared in spin-off versions of the Rocky movie. He has also commentated for ESPN alongside former champion Timothy Bradley.

TRA

CARLOS MONZON

Nicknames	Escopeta
Nationality	Argentine
Weight(s)	Middleweight
Height	1.82 m (6 ft 0 in)
Stance	Orthodox

FIRST FIGHT 1963

RETIRED 1977

TOTAL FIGHTS	100

WINS	WINS BY KO	LOSSES	DRAWS
87	59	3	9

BIOGRAPHY

Carlos Roque Monzon was born on the 7th of August 1942 in Santa Fe, Argentina. Being born and raised in poverty Monzon was required to help provide for his family from a young age. A fan of boxing, Carlos picked up the gloves and turned amateur in the late 1950s. Overall he took part in almost 90 amateur bouts.

With a nickname loosely translated as 'shotgun', Monzon was a wild character away from the ring and a relentless competitor inside of the ropes. Known for setting a quick pace in fights, Monzon fought many times in the early years, mainly in Argentina and in Brazil.

Competing almost every month, often going the 10-round distance, Monzon won the Argentina middleweight title and became South American champion. His consistency led to a world title shot in 1970 and he travelled to Italy to take on unified WBC and WBA champion Nino Benvenuti. It was scheduled for 15 rounds, but Monzon knocked the champion out in the 12th in the Ring Magazine's Fight of the Year.

Benvenuti was a credible champion and Monzon's first defence was a rematch in Monaco. It was nowhere near as competitive as the first fight as Monzon laid a beating on Benvenuti, forcing his manager to throw in the towel. Benvenuti never fought again but Monzon's epic run was only beginning.

He went on to stop former three-time world king Emile Griffith, which was not an easy task given Griffith's toughness and experience. Monzon would later defeat

Griffith again, this time on points.

Carlos also defeated 'Bad' Bennie Briscoe during his reign and, not afraid to go on the road, he twice travelled to France to defeat Jean Claude Bouttier and knocked out Tom Bogs in Denmark.

In a daring jump from welterweight, outstanding champion Jose Napoles was dismissed after six rounds when he tried to step up to middleweight. Aussie Tony Mundine was beaten in seven, and in his final two fights Monzon outpointed Rodrigo Valdes over 15 rounds in back-to-back contests. Both fights were in Monaco and Colombia's Valdes was a dangerous puncher who briefly held the titles after Monzon announced his retirement in August 1977.

During his peak years Monzon was a physically strong fighter who came forward and worked his opponents into submission. His hand speed and punching power made him so difficult to beat.

Fighting over 14 years as a professional, for half of that time Monzon reigned as the undisputed middleweight champion, defending his position on 14 occasions. In 2002 the Ring Magazine ranked Monzon highly in their greatest fighters of all time edition. Monzon lost three times, but they were all early in his career and each one was later avenged.

Away from the ring Monzon was known as a dangerous man with a history of violent behaviour. During his career, however, the entire country would stop and watch his fights. Monzon died in a car accident in 1995. Thousands gathered on the streets for his funeral, chanting the name of their champion.

PERNELL WHITAKER

Nicknames	Sweet Pea
Nationality	American
Weight(s)	Lightweight, Light welterweight, Welterweight, Light middleweight
Height	1.68 m (5 ft 6 in)
Stance	Southpaw

FIRST FIGHT 1984

RETIRED 2001

TOTAL FIGHTS	46

WINS	WINS BY KO	LOSSES	DRAWS
40	17	4	1

BIOGRAPHY

Pernell Whitaker was born on the 2nd of January 1964 in Norfolk, Virginia. Whitaker pulled on the gloves from an early age and had hundreds of amateur contests, many at the highest level. He won lightweight silver at the 1982 World Championships in Munich and gold in the 1983 Pan American Games in Caracas.

This led to his crowning moment at the 1984 Olympic Games in Los Angeles where 'Sweet Pea' won gold, beating Puerto Rican Luis Ortiz in the final.

Turning pro in that same year, Whitaker displayed good punching power early on as he worked through a series of journeymen and gatekeepers. As the levels increased the KOs dried up and Whitaker turned into a slick, defensive mover who could outbox his opponents with ease. Beating Roger Mayweather in 1987 led to a world title shot in 1988 where he was beaten by Jose Luis Ramirez on points.

After suffering his first defeat Whitaker would not lose again for nearly 10 years. He first beat Greg Haugen for the IBF lightweight title before gaining revenge over Ramirez and adding the vacant WBC belt to his cupboard.

Whitaker later picked up the WBA belt from Juan Nazario to become undisputed king of the weight class. A brief stay at super-lightweight gained him a world title in 1992 before a controversial draw against Mexican legend Julio Cesar Chavez at welterweight in 1993. Many believed Whitaker had won the fight by a comfortable margin.

Pernell kept hold of his WBC 147-pound belt and continued defending it until he lost to Oscar De La Hoya in 1997. In his final defence before losing to the 'Golden Boy' Whitaker was in a strange fight against unbeaten Diosbelys Hurtado. Whitaker was showing signs of decline and had been dropped and hurt before he punched Hurtado through the ropes to save the fight.

With his career coming to an end Whitaker began having personal problems, although he managed to go the distance against up-and-coming puncher Felix Trinidad in 1999. When Whitaker lost his final bout by knockout, he was no longer the same fighter and was beaten by a boxer he would never have lost to in his prime.

Pernell had a unique skillset and is recognised as one of the greatest defensive fighters of all time. He was fast and slick, moving out of range, making him extremely difficult to hit. This often led to negative fights that lacked excitement, drawing criticism of Whitaker at times.

Following 17 years in the profession, Whitaker retired as a four-weight world champion, including undisputed and lineal honours. He made numerous defences of his lightweight titles. In 2006 Whitaker was inducted into the International Boxing Hall of Fame at the first attempt.

After finally exiting the ring for good, Whitaker became a trainer. He worked with world champions Zab Judah and Paul Spadafora, as well as prospect Joel Julio and heavyweight contender Calvin Brock. Whitaker died in 2019 when he was struck by a vehicle in his hometown.

TRAP

EVANDER HOLYFIELD

Nicknames	The Real Deal
Nationality	American
Weight(s)	Light heavyweight, Cruiserweight, Heavyweight
Height	1.89 m (6 ft 2 in)
Stance	Orthodox

FIRST FIGHT
1984

RETIRED
2011

TOTAL FIGHTS	57

WINS	WINS BY KO	LOSSES	DRAWS
44	29	10	2

BIOGRAPHY

Evander Holyfield was born on the 19th of October 1962 in Atmore, Alabama. After moving from Alabama at a young age, Holyfield escaped the crime-filled streets of Atlanta, Georgia to box amateur. Winning silver at the 1983 Pan American Games in Venezuela, Evander was selected to represent the United States at the 1984 Olympics where he was controversially disqualified in the semi-final.

Settling for a bronze medal he turned professional, defeating Dwight Muhammad Qawi for a world title at cruiserweight after only 12 fights. Holyfield later knocked out Qawi in a rematch and unified the two remaining belts by beating Ricky Parkey and Carlos DeLeon, before opting to move up for a campaign in boxing's money division.

Often described as being too small for heavyweight, Holyfield made it his mission to fight on even terms with some of boxing's biggest men. After moving up he feasted on some contenders and unbeaten prospect Alex Stewart before knocking out James 'Buster' Douglas for the world heavyweight titles. Douglas had previously shocked the world by knocking out Mike Tyson in Japan.

Holyfield defended against ageing legends George Foreman and Larry Holmes before losing to Riddick Bowe in 1992. Holyfield and Bowe would fight three times in total, with Evander winning the second bout and getting stopped in their third meeting in 1995.

Holyfield fought Mike Tyson twice. He stopped Tyson in their first fight in 1996 and won by disqualification a year later when Tyson bit off his ear. Evander also had two fights apiece with Michael Moorer and Lennox Lewis.

He lost the first fight to Moorer on majority decision in 1994 and stopped him in eight rounds in their 1997 rematch. The first fight with Lewis in early 1999 ended in a controversial draw. Later that year Holyfield lost a close decision to Lennox.

Toward the end of his career Holyfield was still active at world level, boxing the likes of Chris Byrd, John Ruiz and Nikolai Valuev. Aside from Bowe, James Toney was the only other person to knock him out across Holyfield's 27 years as a professional boxer.

Celebrated as a four-time champion, Holyfield is the only fighter during the three-belt era to reign as an undisputed holder in two weight classes. Holding titles across decades, Holyfield is ranked by many publications as the greatest cruiserweight of all time.

Throughout his career Holyfield battled against the odds in the ring as well as medical issues outside of the ropes. In 1994 he was forced to retire due to heart problems. He later returned and would box on for 15 more years.

In 2017, Holyfield's adopted city of Atlanta built a statue of the champion to recognise his sporting contribution. Holyfield also carried the Olympic torch back in 1996 when Atlanta hosted the Games.

Following in the footsteps of George Foreman, Holyfield also released a Real Deal Grill as part of his multiple business interests. Despite making hundreds of millions of dollars across his career, Evander's lifestyle choices have led to money problems.

ARCHIE MOORE

Nicknames	Old Mongoose
Nationality	American
Weight(s)	Light heavyweight, Cruiserweight, Heavyweight
Height	1.80 m (5 ft 11 in)
Stance	Orthodox

FIRST FIGHT
1935

RETIRED
1963

TOTAL FIGHTS	220

WINS	WINS BY KO	LOSSES	DRAWS
186	132	23	10

BIOGRAPHY

Archie Moore was born as Archibald Lee Wright on the 13th of December 1913 in Benoit, Mississippi. Moore had a tough upbringing and was abandoned by his father at a young age, leaving him and his sister to move in with other family members, adopting the surname Moore.

Growing up in segregation, Archie fell into the world of street gangs and brushes with the law that led to a spell in reform school. After catching the boxing bug, Moore is reported to have flitted between amateur and semi-professional contests early on.

Campaigning around middleweight he quickly learned his trade and Moore's fierce punching power set him apart. In 1940 he was based in Australia and won seven bouts, six by knockout before returning to the States.

In 1942 Moore drew with Eddie 'Black Dynamite' Booker for a regional title. He lost to Charley Burley and Ezzard Charles in the late 1940s but kept on pitching towards a world title opportunity. In 1952 Moore outpointed future Hall-of-Famer Joey Maxim to win the light-heavyweight world title. He went on to defeat Maxim twice more before knocking out Harold Johnson and Bobo Olson.

Moore ventured up to heavyweight and mixed with the likes of Rocky Marciano, Floyd Patterson and Muhammad Ali. He was too small to cause any major damage to these champions but remained competitive.

He still dropped back down to defend his light-heavyweight

crown, in London and twice in Canada, winning all those bouts by knockout. Moore was a true throwback fighter who would often travel down to South America or over to Europe to fight in non-title bouts.

Many respected boxing lists hold Moore in high regard. He often appears on best fighters of all-time lists and is one of boxing's greatest finishers, having 132 KOs across a 28-year career. Moore is the longest reigning light-heavyweight champion ever. He was the man to beat for nearly 10 years. That all came after being denied a world title shot for many years due to his colour.

Moore had an impressive style, with moves that were ahead of his era. A good strategist, with excellent defensive instincts, Moore was an accurate puncher with a solid chin. His ability to soak up punishment and avoid shots was an asset for the man known as the 'Old Mongoose' as he regularly fought younger fighters.

Moore was always active in training the youth in boxing, encouraging them to become better people. Although he never moved fully into training professional fighters, he did work with George Foreman and Muhammad Ali, as well as 1980s contender James 'Quick' Tillis who was the first man to take Mike Tyson the distance.

He campaigned politically as a civil rights activist during his long career and made appearances in films and television features. Moore suffered from stomach ulcers during his prime and one operation saw him lose a lot of weight and announce a brief retirement. Archie's daughter Jeanne Marie had two professional contests, in 1997 and 2000, winning both.

TRAF

Joe Frazier

Nicknames	Smokin'
Nationality	American
Weight(s)	Heavyweight
Height	1.81 m (5 ft 11 in)
Stance	Orthodox

First Fight 1965

Retired 1981

Total Fights	37

Wins	Wins by KO	Losses	Draws
32	27	4	1

BIOGRAPHY

Joseph William Frazier was born on the 12th of January 1944 in South Carolina. Frazier was raised in a rural community, working on the farmland. Travelling north to hook up with his brother, young Joe found his way to Philadelphia and into a boxing gym.

Winning the heavyweight Golden Gloves three years in a row, Frazier was on course for the Olympics but first needed to get past rival Buster Mathis. Frazier lost to Mathis in a trial but when the bigger man was injured, Joe took his spot in the 1964 Games. He won a gold medal and exited his amateur career with a reported 38-2 record to become a pro fighter in 1965.

Given his amateur pedigree there was interest in Frazier's potential. Winning his first 11 bouts by KO, Frazier found himself boxing Oscar Bonavena in New York's Madison Square Garden. It was Frazier's toughest bout so far. He was knocked down twice but bounced back to win a split decision.

A string of wins followed as Frazier got past old amateur rival Buster Mathis by KO and contender Jerry Quarry in the 1969 Fight of the Year. He was already a world champion by the time he pulled off his biggest win to date, when he handed Muhammad Ali his first loss, in 1971. Frazier would go on to fight Ali twice more, losing both times. The second bout came in 1974 and the third meeting in 1975, known as 'The Thrilla in Manila'.

By the time of the second Ali fight Frazier had already lost his world title having been brutally knocked out in two rounds by George Foreman in Jamaica. Frazier could never get the better of Foreman and was knocked out in the fifth round of their 1976 rematch. Frazier hung up the gloves after that fight, only to return five years later. Looking older and a lot heavier than his prime weight, Frazier boxed to a draw and never returned to the ring.

Frazier's Philadelphia style made him an extremely difficult opponent. Added to the fact that he was strong, durable, could punch hard and kept coming forward. Frazier wore opponents down with his pressure and he used his powerful left hook to knock people out. 27 of his 32 wins came by KO. Frazier was quite small in stature when compared to some of the huge heavyweights that came after him.

Smokin' Joe received multiple awards across his career and was recognised by the Boxing Writers Association of America and the Ring Magazine as Fighter of the Year on more than one occasion. Reigning as the undisputed heavyweight king from 1970 to 1973 Frazier is often listed in the top 10 of any greatest heavyweight rankings.

An accomplished singer, Frazier formed a band in the 1970s and embarked on a tour across Europe and the United States. Frazier once appeared as himself in an episode of The Simpsons. There is a statue in Philadelphia to celebrate the life and achievements of this boxing hero.

OSCAR DE LA HOYA

Nicknames	Golden Boy
Nationality	American and Mexican
Weight(s)	Super featherweight, Lightweight, Light welterweight, Welterweight, Light middleweight, Middleweight
Height	1.79 m (5 ft 10 in)
Stance	Orthodox

FIRST FIGHT
1992

RETIRED
2008

TOTAL FIGHTS	45

WINS	WINS BY KO	LOSSES	DRAWS
39	30	6	0

BIOGRAPHY

Oscar De La Hoya was born on the 4th of February 1973 in Los Angeles, California. De La Hoya has American Mexican citizenship as his parents emigrated from Mexico before he was born.

Boxing was in De La Hoya's blood, and he enjoyed an excellent amateur career that ended with a gold medal at the 1992 Barcelona Olympics. At this time Oscar's mother was seriously ill and her dying wish was that her son would win the gold medal - which he did.

De La Hoya's medal not only earned him the nickname 'Golden Boy', but he brought back interest in the American boxing scene. Oscar's appeal and personality meant that many new fans followed him throughout his 16 years as a pro.

De La Hoya turned pro in late 1992 and knocked out several early opponents before winning his first world title in 1994. That was the WBO strap at super-featherweight when he made the undefeated champion, Jimmi Bredahl, retire after 10 rounds.

After a single defence De La Hoya moved up to lightweight to win the WBO belt. As the years went by Oscar gradually climbed the weights and started adding notable names to his record. Even though the likes of Julio Cesar Chavez, Pernell Whitaker and Hector Camacho had seen better days, Oscar was building a stronger resume.

He also defeated two quality unbeaten fighters along the way in Miguel Gonzalez and Ike Quartey before running into Felix

Trinidad and suffering his first loss. Shane Mosley was a fighter who always seemed to find a way of beating De La Hoya. They fought twice and Mosley won both times by tight points decisions. De La Hoya's beef with Fernando Vargas was personal and the pair settled the score in 2002 when Oscar knocked out his rival in 11 rounds.

Oscar moved up to middleweight in 2004 but was stopped by Bernard Hopkins with a body shot. At a more natural weight class, Oscar caused Floyd Mayweather trouble before Floyd pulled away to win on points. In his final bout, Oscar boiled down in weight to face the exceptional Manny Pacquiao but lacked the speed and strength to compete.

Oscar won many awards throughout his career, including the Ring Magazine Fighter of the Year for 1995 and he was regularly on pound-for-pound lists. For years De La Hoya was a Pay-Per-View star who was believed to have generated around $700 million in PPV revenue.

De La Hoya had a strong left jab and was famous for his left hook. In the Felix Trinidad fight he was criticised for easing off and moving too much in the final rounds, allowing Trinidad to close the gap and win.

Oscar has always been busy outside of the ropes. He has released a music CD of ballads, been featured on the cover of computer games and authorised a children's picture book.

His charitable foundation helps underprivileged children, especially within Latino communities. Golden Boy Promotions has been one of America's top boxing promotional companies since his retirement.

TRAF

Printed in Great Britain
by Amazon